Adult

MAD LIBS®

The world's greatest _family_ game

Arrested Development Mad Libs

by Kendra Levin and Nico Medina

PRICE STERN SLOAN
An Imprint of Penguin Group (USA) LLC

PRICE STERN SLOAN
Published by the Penguin Group
Penguin Group (USA) LLC, 375 Hudson Street, New York, New York 10014, USA

USA I Canada I UK I Ireland I Australia I New Zealand I India I South Africa I China

penguin.com
A Penguin Random House Company

Mad Libs format copyright © 2015 by Price Stern Sloan,
an imprint of Penguin Group (USA) LLC. All rights reserved.
Arrested Development TM & © 2015 Twentieth Century Fox Film Corporation. All Rights Reserved.

Published by Price Stern Sloan,
a division of Penguin Young Readers Group,
345 Hudson Street, New York, New York 10014.
Printed in the USA.

ISBN 978-0-8431-8259-0

1 3 5 7 9 10 8 6 4 2

MAD LIBS® is a game for people who don't like games!
It can be played by one, two, three, four, or forty.

• RIDICULOUSLY SIMPLE DIRECTIONS

In this book, you'll find stories containing blank spaces where words are left out. One player, the READER, selects one of the stories. The READER shouldn't tell anyone what the story is about. Instead, the READER should ask the other players, the WRITERS, to give words to fill in the blank spaces in the story.

• TO PLAY

The READER asks each WRITER in turn to call out words—adjectives or nouns or whatever the spaces call for—and uses them to fill in the blank spaces in the story. The result is your very own MAD LIBS! Then, when the READER reads the completed MAD LIBS to the other players, they will discover they have written a story that is fantastic, screamingly funny, shocking, silly, crazy, or just plain dumb—depending on the words each WRITER called out.

• EXAMPLE (*Before* and *After*)

" _____ !" he said _____
     EXCLAMATION   ADVERB

as he jumped into his convertible _____ and
                                               NOUN

drove off with his _____ wife.
                              ADJECTIVE

"   *Ouch*   !" he said   *stupidly*
     EXCLAMATION   ADVERB

as he jumped into his convertible   *cat*   and
                                               NOUN

drove off with his   *brave*   wife.
                              ADJECTIVE

In case you have forgotten what adjectives, adverbs, nouns, and verbs are, here is a quick review:

An **ADJECTIVE** describes something or somebody. *Lumpy, soft, ugly, messy,* and *short* are adjectives.

An **ADVERB** tells how something is done. It modifies a verb and usually ends in "ly." *Modestly, stupidly, greedily,* and *carefully* are adverbs.

A **NOUN** is the name of a person, place, or thing. *Sidewalk, umbrella, bridle, bathtub,* and *nose* are nouns.

A **VERB** is an action word. *Run, pitch, jump,* and *swim* are verbs. Put the verbs in past tense if the directions say **PAST TENSE.** *Ran, pitched, jumped,* and *swam* are verbs in the past tense.

When we ask for **A PLACE,** we mean any sort of place: a country or city (*Spain, Cleveland*) or a room (*bathroom, kitchen*).

An **EXCLAMATION** or **SILLY WORD** is any sort of funny sound, gasp, grunt, or outcry, like *Wow!, Ouch!, Whomp!, Ick!,* and *Gadzooks!*

When we ask for specific words, like a **NUMBER,** a **COLOR,** an **ANIMAL,** or a **PART OF THE BODY,** we mean a word that is one of those things, like *seven, blue, horse,* or *head.*

When we ask for a **PLURAL,** it means more than one. For example, *cat* pluralized is *cats.*

MAD LIBS® is fun to play with friends, but you can also play it by yourself! To begin with, DO NOT look at the story on the page below. Fill in the blanks on this page with the words called for. Then, using the words you have selected, fill in the blank spaces in the story. Now you've created your own hilarious MAD LIBS® game!

ADJECTIVE _____

TYPE OF LIQUID _____

PERSON IN ROOM _____

TYPE OF FOOD _____

PLURAL NOUN _____

ADJECTIVE _____

VERB _____

SAME VERB _____

ADJECTIVE _____

OCCUPATION _____

NOUN _____

NOUN _____

VERB (PAST TENSE) _____

NOUN _____

ADVERB _____

VERB ENDING IN "ING" _____

If there's one lesson I've always taught my son, it's that family is the

most _____ thing. I always tell him that blood is thicker
     ADJECTIVE

than _____. You could never eat a whole _____'s
  TYPE OF LIQUID   PERSON IN ROOM

Scramble without your family, and it's no fun using the

_____-baller alone. Twins like Lindsay and I even finish each
  TYPE OF FOOD

other's _____! Family sticks by you, even when you're under
      PLURAL NOUN

investigation for _____ treason. Without family, we wouldn't
         ADJECTIVE

have an attic to _____ in!
        VERB

Of course, if it wasn't for family, we wouldn't need to _____
                                             SAME VERB

in the first place. Or if family had done the _____ thing and
                   ADJECTIVE

made me _____ years ago, the Bluth Company wouldn't
     OCCUPATION

be in trouble. Without family, I wouldn't have to live in a fake

home that's falling into a/an _____-hole, or give my siblings
              NOUN

handouts. Or ride a/an _____ to work. Not to mention how
           NOUN

they've _____ every relationship I've ever had, from Sally
  VERB (PAST TENSE)

Sitwell to my dead _____. That's it. I'm out of this family,
          NOUN

_____. We're _____ to Phoenix.
  ADVERB   VERB ENDING IN "ING"

Adult MAD LIBS®

The world's greatest _family_ game

HOW TO SUCCEED IN BUSINESS, BY GEORGE BLUTH SR.

MAD LIBS® is fun to play with friends, but you can also play it by yourself! To begin with, DO NOT look at the story on the page below. Fill in the blanks on this page with the words called for. Then, using the words you have selected, fill in the blank spaces in the story. Now you've created your own hilarious MAD LIBS® game!

VERB ENDING IN "ING" _____

PART OF THE BODY _____

ADJECTIVE _____

ADJECTIVE _____

PLURAL NOUN _____

PLURAL NOUN _____

NOUN _____

ADJECTIVE _____

NOUN _____

ADJECTIVE _____

NUMBER _____

ADJECTIVE _____

NOUN _____

ADJECTIVE _____

PLURAL NOUN _____

Adult
MAD LIBS
The world's greatest *family* game

HOW TO SUCCEED
IN BUSINESS,
BY GEORGE BLUTH SR.

My kids will tell you that I love _____ lessons. They learned

VERB ENDING IN "ING"

a lot from me and J. Walter Weatherman, my friend with one

_____. But those were simple life lessons. My expertise

PART OF THE BODY

lies in business, and I'm here to give you some _____ wisdom:

ADJECTIVE

- Investments are nice, but nothing beats _____, hard cash.

ADJECTIVE

  Line the _____ of your place of business with dollar

PLURAL NOUN

  bills, but watch out for _____.

PLURAL NOUN

- Faith is a/an _____. But don't let _____ belief

NOUN ADJECTIVE

  systems get in your way. Practice whatever religion best suits you

  and your _____ at the time.

NOUN

- Make 'em sweat. You get a man hot and _____ enough,

ADJECTIVE

  and he'll pay you _____ dollars just for a glass of lemonade.

NUMBER

- Hire a loyal assistant with _____ self-esteem but never

ADJECTIVE

  promise her a/an _____!

NOUN

- And finally, find yourself a/an _____ lawyer. My guy told

ADJECTIVE

  me years ago to conduct all my business _____ at sea.

PLURAL NOUN

  He's very good.

MAD LIBS® is fun to play with friends, but you can also play it by yourself! To begin with, DO NOT look at the story on the page below. Fill in the blanks on this page with the words called for. Then, using the words you have selected, fill in the blank spaces in the story. Now you've created your own hilarious MAD LIBS® game!

SILLY WORD _____

ADJECTIVE _____

A PLACE _____

ADVERB _____

NOUN _____

ADJECTIVE _____

PERSON IN ROOM (MALE) _____

NOUN _____

ADJECTIVE _____

PLURAL NOUN _____

PART OF THE BODY _____

VERB _____

ADJECTIVE _____

NOUN _____

PART OF THE BODY (PLURAL) _____

ADJECTIVE _____

ADJECTIVE _____

MICHAEL AND WOMEN?

Poor Michael Bluth doesn't have the best luck with the ladies. For

years after his wife died, Michael—who had only had _____

SILLY WORD

with four women—devoted himself to raising his son. But when

_____-relations expert Jessie Bowers said it was time he

ADJECTIVE

start dating, Michael thought he'd give it a try. (His mother and

sister then roughed Jessie up in a fancy _____, so that

A PLACE

relationship ended _____.) Michael briefly dated his son's

ADVERB

teacher Miss Baerly, but it turned out George Michael had a/an

_____ on her, and she had a/an _____ obsession

NOUN   ADJECTIVE

with _____ Hussein. Spanish _____-opera

PERSON IN ROOM (MALE)   NOUN

star Marta was _____ for Michael, but his _____

ADJECTIVE   PLURAL NOUN

had feelings for her, too. And who could forget Maggie Lizer—as

in "lies her _____ off"—who convinced Michael

PART OF THE BODY

she couldn't _____? Rita Leeds of _____ Britain

VERB   ADJECTIVE

had the _____ of a child, and Michael fell head over

NOUN

_____ for her. But love, like justice, is _____,

PART OF THE BODY (PLURAL)   ADJECTIVE

for Rita had a secret: She was a mentally _____ female.

ADJECTIVE

Come on!

Adult
MAD LIBS®

The world's greatest _family_ game

THE ART OF SEDUCTION, BY G.O.B.

MAD LIBS® is fun to play with friends, but you can also play it by yourself! To begin with, DO NOT look at the story on the page below. Fill in the blanks on this page with the words called for. Then, using the words you have selected, fill in the blank spaces in the story. Now you've created your own hilarious MAD LIBS® game!

VERB _____

ADVERB _____

ANIMAL (PLURAL) _____

NOUN _____

PLURAL NOUN _____

NOUN _____

ANIMAL _____

VERB ENDING IN "ING" _____

NOUN _____

LETTER OF THE ALPHABET _____

NOUN _____

NOUN _____

ADJECTIVE _____

VERB (PAST TENSE) _____

VERB _____

NOUN _____

Adult MAD LIBS®

THE ART OF SEDUCTION, BY G.O.B.

The world's greatest _family_ game

When it comes to the ladies, I always get what I _____ .
                                                    VERB

Whether I'm wooing a TV star, a/an _____ legal teenager,
                                        ADVERB

or one of the _____ that Michael dates, I've never heard
                ANIMAL (PLURAL)

any complaints. Here are a few tips that have helped me lay my

_____ upon their sweet _____:
   NOUN   PLURAL NOUN

- **Women love magicians.** If you can make a/an _____
                                                      NOUN

  come out of your sleeve or pull a/an _____ out of a hat,
                                            ANIMAL

  you'll be _____ them off with a stick. And remember, it's
              VERB ENDING IN "ING"

  not a/an _____—it's an illusion!
             NOUN

- **Women love boats.** When I lived on the _____
                                              LETTER OF THE ALPHABET

  Word, it was a total _____ magnet.
                           NOUN

- **Women love puppets**, which is why I always bring my

  _____, Franklin, along on dates. There's nothing like a
     NOUN

  little _____ racial humor to loosen up your lady.
          ADJECTIVE

- **Women love _me_**, so good luck, guy. I've _____ most
                                                 VERB (PAST TENSE)

  of them already, and if I find out there's one you like, I'll

  _____ her, too. That's just the kind of _____ I am.
     VERB   NOUN

From ADULT MAD LIBS®: Arrested Development Mad Libs • Arrested Development TM & © 2015 Twentieth Century Fox Film Corporation.
All Rights Reserved. Published by Price Stern Sloan, an imprint of Penguin Group (USA) LLC, 345 Hudson Street, New York, NY 10014.

Adult MAD LIBS®

The world's greatest _family_ game

I CARE DEEPLY FOR...
WHATEVER,
BY LINDSAY BLUTH FÜNKE

MAD LIBS® is fun to play with friends, but you can also play it by yourself! To begin with, DO NOT look at the story on the page below. Fill in the blanks on this page with the words called for. Then, using the words you have selected, fill in the blank spaces in the story. Now you've created your own hilarious MAD LIBS® game!

ADJECTIVE _____

VERB _____

PART OF THE BODY (PLURAL) _____

CELEBRITY _____

A PLACE _____

NUMBER _____

ANIMAL _____

PLURAL NOUN _____

NOUN _____

ADJECTIVE _____

NOUN _____

VERB _____

A PLACE _____

NOUN _____

ADVERB _____

NOUN _____

NOUN _____

ADJECTIVE _____

Adult
MAD LIBS
The world's greatest _family_ game

I CARE DEEPLY FOR . . .
WHATEVER,
BY LINDSAY BLUTH FÜNKE

I like to think of myself as a/an _____ activist, someone
_{ADJECTIVE}

who's always ready to _____ a sign or flash her
_{VERB}

gorgeous _____ for a good cause. When we had
_{PART OF THE BODY (PLURAL)}

more money than _____, I threw fundraisers that were the
_{CELEBRITY}

envy of every socialite in (the) _____. I once brought in
_{A PLACE}

over _____ dollars for my anti-circumcision charity. (As I
_{NUMBER}

always say, it's a/an _____—let it have its _____!) I
_{ANIMAL} _{PLURAL NOUN}

protested fishing, _____ cruelty, and school lunches—oops,
_{NOUN}

I mean I _supported_ school lunches—and saved the _____-
_{ADJECTIVE}

lands. I even lived in a/an _____ with a really gross guy until
_{NOUN}

I realized I'd have to _____ in a bucket. But my most worthy
_{VERB}

cause came when I found out my hairdresser was going to fight in

(the) _____. I whipped out my _____, hurried down
_{A PLACE} _{NOUN}

to the army base, and _____ chanted, "No _____ for
_{ADVERB} _{NOUN}

oil!" I don't want to brag, but it was truly my finest _____—
_{NOUN}

and my hair had never looked more _____.
_{ADJECTIVE}

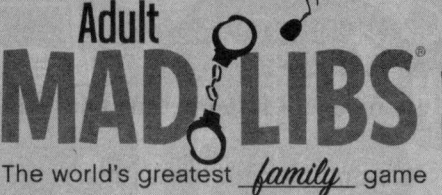

MAD LIBS® is fun to play with friends, but you can also play it by yourself! To begin with, DO NOT look at the story on the page below. Fill in the blanks on this page with the words called for. Then, using the words you have selected, fill in the blank spaces in the story. Now you've created your own hilarious MAD LIBS® game!

ADJECTIVE _____

NOUN _____

TYPE OF FOOD _____

NOUN _____

PART OF THE BODY (PLURAL) _____

SILLY WORD _____

ADJECTIVE _____

TYPE OF FOOD _____

NOUN _____

ARTICLE OF CLOTHING _____

NOUN _____

NUMBER _____

VERB (PAST TENSE) _____

NUMBER _____

ADJECTIVE _____

TYPE OF LIQUID _____

VERB _____

Adult MAD LIBS®

WHAT I LOVE ABOUT MOTHER, BY BUSTER BLUTH

The world's greatest _family_ game

Mom's _____. She's a sassy _____ who can serve
     ADJECTIVE   NOUN

up a mean bowl of _____, all while taking a drag from
               TYPE OF FOOD

her _____. And just look at the _____ on
    NOUN   PART OF THE BODY (PLURAL)

her—_____! Sure, sometimes she can get off on being
      SILLY WORD

_____. She's gotten me with the old _____ trick many
  ADJECTIVE   TYPE OF FOOD

times. She always makes me stand on the _____ while she puts
                        NOUN

on her _____, and yet anything goes at _____-time!
   ARTICLE OF CLOTHING   NOUN

When the doctor said I couldn't see her for _____ weeks after
                        NUMBER

she got her face _____, I was like, "Make it _____
      VERB (PAST TENSE)   NUMBER

weeks!" But in spite of her _____ personality and fondness
                  ADJECTIVE

for _____, I _____ Mom. Maybe we should call her.
  TYPE OF LIQUID   VERB

MAD LIBS® is fun to play with friends, but you can also play it by yourself! To begin with, DO NOT look at the story on the page below. Fill in the blanks on this page with the words called for. Then, using the words you have selected, fill in the blank spaces in the story.

Now you've created your own hilarious MAD LIBS® game!

PERSON IN ROOM _____

PLURAL NOUN _____

NOUN _____

ADJECTIVE _____

ADJECTIVE _____

PLURAL NOUN _____

PART OF THE BODY _____

ANIMAL _____

ADJECTIVE _____

NUMBER _____

NOUN _____

ADJECTIVE _____

ADVERB _____

ADJECTIVE _____

COLOR _____

VERB _____

NOUN _____

When I was chief of psychiatry at _____ Memorial
<small>PERSON IN ROOM</small>

Hospital, I treated many _____ and became the first
<small>PLURAL NOUN</small>

anal-_____ in the field. But nothing in my medical career
<small>NOUN</small>

prepared me for the _____ life of an actor. When I first
<small>ADJECTIVE</small>

discovered the theater, I was _____ for fame. I could taste
<small>ADJECTIVE</small>

those leading-man _____ in my mouth! But in this business
<small>PLURAL NOUN</small>

of show, you must have the _____ of a lion and the
<small>PART OF THE BODY</small>

hide of a/an _____. And you must be prepared to play any
<small>ANIMAL</small>

kind of character, from _____ Inmate #2 to Confidence
<small>ADJECTIVE</small>

Man #_____. Of course, you may discover, as I did, that
<small>NUMBER</small>

the _____ of the theater can be _____ and that
<small>NOUN</small> <small>ADJECTIVE</small>

performance art suits you more _____. Who knows—if
<small>ADVERB</small>

you're _____ and work hard, you just might _____
<small>ADJECTIVE</small> <small>COLOR</small>

yourself. Now that's the way to _____ your dreams and act
<small>VERB</small>

like a real _____!
<small>NOUN</small>

Adult MAD LIBS®

GEORGE MICHAEL: MISTER MANAGER

The world's greatest _family_ game

MAD LIBS® is fun to play with friends, but you can also play it by yourself! To begin with, DO NOT look at the story on the page below. Fill in the blanks on this page with the words called for. Then, using the words you have selected, fill in the blank spaces in the story. Now you've created your own hilarious MAD LIBS® game!

ADJECTIVE _____

NOUN _____

NOUN _____

VERB _____

ADJECTIVE _____

ADJECTIVE _____

ADJECTIVE _____

COLOR _____

NOUN _____

VERB _____

NOUN BEGINNING WITH "F" _____

PLURAL NOUN _____

ADJECTIVE _____

ADVERB _____

NOUN _____

You probably think you know the history of the Bluth Frozen Banana

Stand. My dad told me that in the sixties, all the _____ kids
ADJECTIVE

used to hang out at the "Big Yellow _____" to smoke the
NOUN

marijuana like a/an _____. Now it's where I _____ all
NOUN VERB

day long. I'm Mister Manager, and I've learned a lot from managing

the stand. Marketing is very important. You need a/an _____
ADJECTIVE

slogan like "A Frozen Banana That _Won't_ Make You _____
ADJECTIVE

and Kill You." Being _____ at math is also essential, even
ADJECTIVE

if it means studying until your eyes are _____. I take my
COLOR

_____ very seriously. Grown-ups are allowed to have fun,
NOUN

but kids are supposed to _____. After all, as Jack Welch says,
VERB

_____ and "failure" start with the same letter. But being
NOUN BEGINNING WITH "F"

Mister Manager has its perks, like meeting cute _____ like
PLURAL NOUN

Ann, my girlfriend, who's really _____. And of course, like
ADJECTIVE

Pop-Pop _____ says, there's always _____ in the
ADVERB NOUN

banana stand!

Adult MAD LIBS

The world's greatest _family_ game

GETTING YOUR PARENTS TO NOTICE YOU, BY MAEBY FÜNKE

MAD LIBS® is fun to play with friends, but you can also play it by yourself! To begin with, DO NOT look at the story on the page below. Fill in the blanks on this page with the words called for. Then, using the words you have selected, fill in the blank spaces in the story. Now you've created your own hilarious MAD LIBS® game!

PLURAL NOUN _____

ADVERB _____

PART OF THE BODY (PLURAL) _____

ADJECTIVE _____

NOUN _____

OCCUPATION _____

COLOR _____

A PLACE _____

LETTER OF THE ALPHABET _____

NUMBER _____

NUMBER _____

NOUN _____

PLURAL NOUN _____

PLURAL NOUN _____

NUMBER _____

Adult MAD LIBS

The world's greatest _family_ game

GETTING YOUR PARENTS TO NOTICE YOU, BY MAEBY FÜNKE

If you're like me, and your mom and dad are too wrapped up in their

own _____ to notice you exist, you could _____ use
   PLURAL NOUN   ADVERB

some of my advice.

- Try giving your cousin a kiss on the _____. It'll
                                      PART OF THE BODY (PLURAL)

  really freak your parents out.

- Say you have a/an _____ disease, like BS or Graft-Versus-
                         ADJECTIVE

  _____. Oh wait, that's a real one.
   NOUN

- Con your way into a job as a/an _____. If they don't
                               OCCUPATION

  notice you're not going to school every day, maybe seeing your

  name on the _____ screen will make them wonder.
             COLOR

- Get kicked out of (the) _____. Getting all _____s
                A PLACE   LETTER OF THE ALPABET

  on your report card will make this pretty easy.

- If that doesn't work, try repeating your senior year _____
                                        NUMBER

  times until you're _____ years old. And throw in a
                     NUMBER

  count of statutory _____ while you're at it.
                        NOUN

- Good luck! I'm going to go drown my _____ with about
                                   PLURAL NOUN

  _____ Virgin Marys now . . .
   NUMBER

MAD LIBS® is fun to play with friends, but you can also play it by yourself! To begin with, DO NOT look at the story on the page below. Fill in the blanks on this page with the words called for. Then, using the words you have selected, fill in the blank spaces in the story.

Now you've created your own hilarious MAD LIBS® game!

NOUN _____

NOUN _____

NOUN _____

ADJECTIVE _____

ADVERB _____

PLURAL NOUN _____

ADJECTIVE _____

ADJECTIVE _____

NOUN _____

VERB ENDING IN "ING" _____

A PLACE _____

NUMBER _____

VERB _____

PERSON IN ROOM (MALE) _____

Adult
MAD LIBS®
The world's greatest *family* game

BARRY ZUCKERKORN, ATTORNEY AT LAW: A TV COMMERCIAL

Looking for the perfect offshore tax _____? Barry says, "Take

to the _____!"
    _{NOUN}

_{NOUN}

Arrested for a/an _____ **you didn't commit?** "Tell 'em they
      _{NOUN}

got the _____ twin!"
   _{ADJECTIVE}

Gotta go to trial? "I always show up _____ prepared.
                _{ADVERB}

Especially if it's Ping!"

Barry's experience and _____ cannot be matched. And
              _{PLURAL NOUN}

dozens of _____ clients agree!
     _{ADJECTIVE}

"He's very _____," says Lucille Bluth. Titan of _____
     _{ADJECTIVE}   _{NOUN}

George Bluth says: "I've got the worst _____ attorney."
                _{VERB ENDING IN "ING"}

From (the) _____ to the City of Industry, Barry's got you
      _{A PLACE}

covered.

"One time, he offered me _____ bucks just to _____
        _{NUMBER}   _{VERB}

with him," says local cross-dresser _____. "And this wasn't
           _{PERSON IN ROOM (MALE)}

even in L.A.!"

Adult MAD LIBS

CAGED WISDOM: TIPS ABOUT LIFE IN PRISON

The world's greatest _family_ game

MAD LIBS® is fun to play with friends, but you can also play it by yourself! To begin with, DO NOT look at the story on the page below. Fill in the blanks on this page with the words called for. Then, using the words you have selected, fill in the blank spaces in the story. Now you've created your own hilarious MAD LIBS® game!

PLURAL NOUN _____

ADJECTIVE _____

PART OF THE BODY_____

VERB _____

NOUN _____

NOUN _____

VERB _____

ADVERB _____

NOUN _____

TYPE OF FOOD (PLURAL) _____

ADJECTIVE _____

VERB _____

NOUN _____

NOUN _____

George Sr.: Let faith guide you. When I was trying to decide which gang to join, everyone made a lot of _____. I felt like the
<small>PLURAL NOUN</small>

most _____ girl at the dance! But in the end, I had to follow
<small>ADJECTIVE</small>

the _____ God gave me.
<small>PART OF THE BODY</small>

G.O.B.: Be prepared. You never know when you might need a

key to _____ handcuffs, a/an _____ to climb down
<small>VERB</small> <small>NOUN</small>

the prison walls, or even a glove for a game of _____. And
<small>NOUN</small>

don't forget to _____ a few "forget-me-nows"!
<small>VERB</small>

Lucille: Watch your back. No matter how _____ you've
<small>ADVERB</small>

wormed your way into a Chinese gang, you could still get

shanghaied (look, I made a pun!) by a homicidal _____
<small>NOUN</small>

with a handful of sharpened _____.
<small>TYPE OF FOOD (PLURAL)</small>

Tobias: Keep your spirits up, you _____ tyke! You never know
<small>ADJECTIVE</small>

when circumstances will _____ in your favor. And don't forget
<small>VERB</small>

that somewhere over the rainbow, there's another _____.
<small>NOUN</small>

Barry Zuckerkorn: Have the _____ of your life!
<small>NOUN</small>

Adult MAD LIBS

I'M OSCAR! DOT COM!

The world's greatest _family_ game

MAD LIBS® is fun to play with friends, but you can also play it by yourself! To begin with, DO NOT look at the story on the page below. Fill in the blanks on this page with the words called for. Then, using the words you have selected, fill in the blank spaces in the story. Now you've created your own hilarious MAD LIBS® game!

COLOR _____

VERB _____

ADJECTIVE _____

TYPE OF FOOD _____

TYPE OF LIQUID _____

VERB ENDING IN "ING" _____

ADJECTIVE _____

PLURAL NOUN _____

NOUN _____

PART OF THE BODY (PLURAL) _____

NOUN _____

NOUN _____

TYPE OF FOOD _____

VERB ENDING IN "ING" _____

VERB ENDING IN "ING" _____

ANIMAL _____

ANIMAL _____

Entry #41, _____ County Prison:

COLOR

I can't _____ in prison another day! Oh, how I miss my

VERB

_____ trailer. If only I could go back to my _____

ADJECTIVE TYPE OF FOOD

grove, I would make batch after batch of _____ and never

TYPE OF LIQUID

complain again about _____ all those lemons.

VERB ENDING IN "ING"

The conditions here are _____. Every night in the showers,

ADJECTIVE

they cover their _____ with _____, and you're

PLURAL NOUN NOUN

supposed to thank them!

I wish someone would visit me. What I would give to lay my

_____ on my lady love Lucille, or my son—I mean,

PART OF THE BODY (PLURAL)

my _____—Buster. If only G.O.B. could smuggle in some

NOUN

Afternoon _____ for me in a/an _____, I could

NOUN TYPE OF FOOD

escape . . . at least in my mind.

The stress is _____ me. My hair has stopped _____.

VERB ENDING IN "ING" VERB ENDING IN "ING"

I used to have the hair of a/an _____. Now I'm as bald as

ANIMAL

a/an _____, and everyone thinks I'm my twin brother,

ANIMAL

George! But I'm Oscar! Dot Com!

Adult
MAD LIBS®

AY AY AY, LOS BLUTHS LOCOS! BY LUPE

The world's greatest _family_ game

MAD LIBS® is fun to play with friends, but you can also play it by yourself! To begin with, DO NOT look at the story on the page below. Fill in the blanks on this page with the words called for. Then, using the words you have selected, fill in the blank spaces in the story. Now you've created your own hilarious MAD LIBS® game!

ADJECTIVE _____

A PLACE _____

ADJECTIVE _____

NOUN _____

TYPE OF LIQUID _____

VERB _____

ARTICLE OF CLOTHING _____

VERB ENDING IN "ING" _____

NOUN _____

ADJECTIVE _____

PART OF THE BODY _____

ADJECTIVE _____

NOUN _____

ADVERB _____

NOUN _____

ANIMAL (PLURAL) _____

ADJECTIVE _____

NOUN _____

Adult MAD LIBS®

The world's greatest _family_ game

AY AY AY, LOS BLUTHS LOCOS! BY LUPE

_Ay ay ay_, I work for the most _____ family in all of (the)
                                  ADJECTIVE

_____: _los_ Bluths! At first, it was only _la madre_ I had to deal
A PLACE

with—cleaning her _____ penthouse, letting her check my
                     ADJECTIVE

_____ at the end of each day, and washing all her _____
NOUN   TYPE OF LIQUID

glasses. Then, her daughter, Lindsay, made me _____ her laundry
                                              VERB

(and I couldn't tell her _____ from Mister's!). When I found
                         ARTICLE OF CLOTHING

Buster _____ under my _____, I was so _____
       VERB ENDING IN "ING"   NOUN   ADJECTIVE

I wanted to scream! Then I felt sorry for him when he lost his

_____, and I tried to make him feel _____. But when _la_
PART OF THE BODY   ADJECTIVE

madre caught us making _____ in her old stirrup pants, Buster
                         NOUN

_____ turned against me. Michael is the only Bluth who's
ADVERB

ever treated me like a/an _____—and he sent my family to an
                          NOUN

island full of _____! Still, as _loco_ as _los_ Bluths are, I am grateful
               ANIMAL (PLURAL)

to them for one thing: my stories about their _____ ways have
                                              ADJECTIVE

made me the most popular _____ in my neighborhood.
                         NOUN

Adult
MAD LIBS®
A REVIEW OF KLIMPY'S, BY LUCILLE BLUTH

The world's greatest _family_ game

MAD LIBS® is fun to play with friends, but you can also play it by yourself! To begin with, DO NOT look at the story on the page below. Fill in the blanks on this page with the words called for. Then, using the words you have selected, fill in the blank spaces in the story. Now you've created your own hilarious MAD LIBS® game!

ADJECTIVE _____

VERB ENDING IN "ING" _____

ADJECTIVE _____

TYPE OF LIQUID _____

ADJECTIVE _____

ADJECTIVE _____

ARTICLE OF CLOTHING _____

VERB _____

VERB _____

PERSON IN ROOM _____

PERSON IN ROOM _____

NOUN _____

ADJECTIVE _____

NUMBER _____

VERB _____

Adult MAD LIBS

A REVIEW OF KLIMPY'S, BY LUCILLE BLUTH

The world's greatest _family_ game

I'll only go to this _____ establishment if my blood sugar is

ADJECTIVE

_____ to a/an _____ low. But a woman can't live

VERB ENDING IN "ING"   ADJECTIVE

on _____ alone, so I found myself there last night with my

TYPE OF LIQUID

_____ daughter, Lindsay. We were greeted at the door by a/an

ADJECTIVE

_____ hostess, who wore a yellow _____ and told us

ADJECTIVE   ARTICLE OF CLOTHING

to _____ anywhere we'd like. I had one thought: _This does not_

VERB

_____ _well._ I ordered the _____ and _____

VERB   PERSON IN ROOM   PERSON IN ROOM

Tuna. When asked if I preferred the plate or the platter, I didn't

understand the _____, and I didn't respond to it. It's a good

NOUN

thing the place had a/an _____ bar.

ADJECTIVE

My rating: _____ stars. But if I still had money, I'd buy a

NUMBER

Klimpy's just to _____ it to the ground.

VERB

MAD LIBS® is fun to play with friends, but you can also play it by yourself! To begin with, DO NOT look at the story on the page below. Fill in the blanks on this page with the words called for. Then, using the words you have selected, fill in the blank spaces in the story. Now you've created your own hilarious MAD LIBS® game!

PLURAL NOUN _____

CELEBRITY (MALE) _____

NOUN _____

VERB ENDING IN "ING" _____

ADJECTIVE _____

PLURAL NOUN _____

NOUN _____

SAME NOUN _____

ADVERB _____

SAME ADVERB _____

PART OF THE BODY _____

ADJECTIVE _____

PART OF THE BODY (PLURAL) _____

NOUN _____

ADJECTIVE _____

NUMBER _____

NOUN _____

I used to change Buster's _____ when he was a baby. But

PLURAL NOUN

the night I saw him at the Daytime _____ Awards, it was

CELEBRITY (MALE)

like I was seeing him for the first time. Buster was good for me. My

_____ improved, and for the first time in years, I felt like

NOUN

I was _____ on _____ ground. Once, he tried to

VERB ENDING IN "ING"   ADJECTIVE

buy illegal _____ to help me with my _____ (which

PLURAL NOUN   NOUN

he called _our_ _____). Our romance was _____,

SAME NOUN   ADVERB

_____ grand! But alas, the _____ moves on . . . and

SAME ADVERB   PART OF THE BODY

move on I did. G.O.B. had the most _____ voice. I could

ADJECTIVE

listen to him read the clubhouse menu all day—he made chicken

_____ in _____ sauce sound so intoxicating!

PART OF THE BODY (PLURAL)   NOUN

But when G.O.B. became too _____, I had to end things.

ADJECTIVE

I needed a man, not a boy! By the time Michael hit on me at the

_____ de Cuatro festival, I'd had enough. No more Bluth

NUMBER

boys for this foolish, funny, needy _____!

NOUN

MAD LIBS® is fun to play with friends, but you can also play it by yourself! To begin with, DO NOT look at the story on the page below. Fill in the blanks on this page with the words called for. Then, using the words you have selected, fill in the blank spaces in the story.

Now you've created your own hilarious MAD LIBS® game!

NOUN _____

A PLACE _____

ADJECTIVE _____

ADJECTIVE _____

VERB ENDING IN "ING" _____

ADJECTIVE _____

PLURAL NOUN _____

PART OF THE BODY _____

ADJECTIVE _____

VERB _____

PLURAL NOUN _____

PLURAL NOUN _____

ADJECTIVE _____

VERB ENDING IN "ING" _____

ADJECTIVE _____

NUMBER _____

PLURAL NOUN _____

NUMBER _____

Adult MAD LIBS®

The world's greatest _family_ game

"THE THRIFTY ACTOR": A SEMINAR WITH CARL WEATHERS

Class Summary: In this continuing-education _____ offered
<u>NOUN</u>

at (the) _____ University, _____ actor Carl Weathers
<u>A PLACE</u> <u>ADJECTIVE</u>

provides you with _____ information about _____ in
<u>ADJECTIVE</u> <u>VERB ENDING IN "ING"</u>

the entertainment industry.

Session One: Sustenance: Get your stew on! Learn what items from

craft services make the most _____ stews, how to stretch your
<u>ADJECTIVE</u>

per diem to its fullest, and which restaurants offer the most generous

_____ to staff.
<u>PLURAL NOUN</u>

Session Two: Transportation: Getting around town doesn't have to

cost you an arm and a/an _____! Carl Weathers knows all the
<u>PART OF THE BODY</u>

_____ ways to the airport, and how to _____ the airline
<u>ADJECTIVE</u> <u>VERB</u>

industry. He also buys all his _____ at police _____—
<u>PLURAL NOUN</u> <u>PLURAL NOUN</u>

he's full of _____ stuff like that!
<u>ADJECTIVE</u>

**Bonus Session: Stage _____: _____-hitting star of
<u>VERB ENDING IN "ING"</u> <u>ADJECTIVE</u>

Rocky _____ reveals his trade secrets. Put up your _____!
<u>NUMBER</u> <u>PLURAL NOUN</u>

Course Fee: Only got _____ dollars? Well, that's _just_ what this
<u>NUMBER</u>

course costs!

From ADULT MAD LIBS®: Arrested Development Mad Libs • Arrested Development TM & © 2015 Twentieth Century Fox Film Corporation.
All Rights Reserved. Published by Price Stern Sloan, an imprint of Penguin Group (USA) LLC, 345 Hudson Street, New York, NY 10014.

The world's greatest _family_ game

MAD LIBS® is fun to play with friends, but you can also play it by yourself! To begin with, DO NOT look at the story on the page below. Fill in the blanks on this page with the words called for. Then, using the words you have selected, fill in the blank spaces in the story. Now you've created your own hilarious MAD LIBS® game!

ADJECTIVE _____

NOUN _____

ANIMAL _____

NOUN _____

PERSON IN ROOM _____

PART OF THE BODY _____

PLURAL NOUN _____

NOUN _____

VERB ENDING IN "ING" _____

NOUN _____

ADJECTIVE _____

ADJECTIVE _____

NOUN _____

VERB _____

Dear Mother,

Army is _____. I was surprised they let me join, with my night
       ADJECTIVE

blindness, my _____ attacks, and the fact that my Linus is
       NOUN

shaped like a/an _____ tail without its _____, but I
       ANIMAL   NOUN

guess they're desperate. Today Sgt. _____ called me a candy
       PERSON IN ROOM

ass and told me to get my head out of my _____!
       PART OF THE BODY

Next week we have half a day, so I may come home to show you my

_____. I got a/an _____ for marksmanship and a
  PLURAL NOUN   NOUN

seal for sand-_____. Soon they want to put me in something
     VERB ENDING IN "ING"

called _____ squad. Even though you only signed me up
     NOUN

because the _____ man dared you to, I'm glad I'm in Army. If
     ADJECTIVE

things keep going well, I could even go to war just like Uncle Oscar.

It's _____ how alike he and I are!
   ADJECTIVE

Gotta go—it's time for _____ practice. I _____ you,
       NOUN   VERB

Mother.

Love,

Buster

MAD LIBS® is fun to play with friends, but you can also play it by yourself! To begin with, DO NOT look at the story on the page below. Fill in the blanks on this page with the words called for. Then, using the words you have selected, fill in the blank spaces in the story. Now you've created your own hilarious MAD LIBS® game!

TYPE OF FOOD _____

NOUN _____

NOUN _____

ADJECTIVE _____

ADJECTIVE _____

A PLACE _____

NOUN _____

ADJECTIVE _____

TYPE OF FOOD _____

PART OF THE BODY _____

NUMBER _____

ADJECTIVE _____

VERB ENDING IN "ING" _____

ANIMAL _____

NOUN _____

NOUN _____

NOUN _____

HER?

The world's greatest _family_ game

Just what do we know about Ann? . . . *Who?* You know—Ann

_____! George Michael's first _____. Oh, *her*!
　　　TYPE OF FOOD　　　　　　　　　　　　　　　　　　NOUN

Well . . . her body's shaped like a/an _____ and she has
　　　　　　　　　　　　　　　　　　　NOUN

a/an _____ center of gravity. She's _____ about God. She
　　　ADJECTIVE　　　　　　　　　　　　　ADJECTIVE

celebrates Christmas on (the) _____ time. Protesting a French
　　　　　　　　　　　　　A PLACE

film or a TV _____ makes her _____, even if it's a satire.
　　　　　　NOUN　　　　　　　　　ADJECTIVE

She is the inventor of the Mayon-_____, which she makes in
　　　　　　　　　　　　　　TYPE OF FOOD

her _____. She finished in the top _____ at
　　PART OF THE BODY　　　　　　　　　　　　　　NUMBER

a/an _____ beauty pageant. Her talent was _____
　　　ADJECTIVE　　　　　　　　　　　　　　　VERB ENDING IN "ING"

with a/an _____. That's where she met George Michael's
　　　　　ANIMAL

uncle G.O.B., with whom she later had _____. They became
　　　　　　　　　　　　　　　　　　　NOUN

engaged, but G.O.B. left her at the _____. She later had a/an
　　　　　　　　　　　　　　　　NOUN

_____ with magician Tony Wonder.
　NOUN

Really, Tony? *Her?*

Adult

MAD LIBS®

ASK "I CAN!" WITH STEVE HOLT

The world's greatest _family_ game

MAD LIBS® is fun to play with friends, but you can also play it by yourself! To begin with, DO NOT look at the story on the page below. Fill in the blanks on this page with the words called for. Then, using the words you have selected, fill in the blank spaces in the story. Now you've created your own hilarious MAD LIBS® game!

NOUN _____

ADVERB _____

PLURAL NOUN _____

ADJECTIVE _____

NOUN _____

LETTER OF THE ALPHABET _____

PLURAL NOUN _____

ADJECTIVE _____

ANIMAL _____

OCCUPATION _____

NOUN _____

TYPE OF LIQUID _____

NOUN _____

ADJECTIVE _____

Adult MAD LIBS®

ASK "I CAN!" WITH STEVE HOLT

The world's greatest _family_ game

When I was elected student _____ president for the seventh time,

NOUN

people asked me, "Steve Holt, how do you do it?" I _____ replied,

ADVERB

"Steve Holt!" But since you asked, here are a few of my _____ :

PLURAL NOUN

- **STAY FIT!** The _____ Greeks believed in a sound mind and

ADJECTIVE

  a/an _____ body, so make exercise a regular part of your

ADJECTIVE

  _____ . Remember, there is no _____ in "win!"

NOUN   LETTER OF THE ALPHABET

- **NEVER GIVE UP!** Whether you're trying out for the lead in

  the school play or working hard to build a career exterminating

  _____ , believe in yourself and keep going. You can

PLURAL NOUN

  control your bladder when you're _____ !

ADJECTIVE

- **DON'T BE A/AN _____ !** The search for my father was

ANIMAL

  full of uncertainty. Who would he be—an explorer, an astronaut,

  a/an _____ ? Or a magician who couldn't even pull a/

OCCUPATION

  an _____ out of his pants without squirting _____

NOUN   TYPE OF LIQUID

  everywhere? And what man would get my mom pregnant and then,

  when I try to find him, hide like a/an _____ ? These were

NOUN

  tough questions, but I had one _____ answer: STEVE HOLT!

ADJECTIVE

MAD LIBS® is fun to play with friends, but you can also play it by yourself! To begin with, DO NOT look at the story on the page below. Fill in the blanks on this page with the words called for. Then, using the words you have selected, fill in the blank spaces in the story. Now you've created your own hilarious MAD LIBS® game!

TYPE OF FOOD _____

ADJECTIVE _____

NOUN _____

VERB (PAST TENSE) _____

NUMBER _____

OCCUPATION _____

NOUN _____

NOUN _____

ADVERB _____

ADJECTIVE _____

ADJECTIVE _____

NOUN _____

ADJECTIVE _____

VERB _____

PLURAL NOUN _____

Did somebody say "Wonder"? Pay no attention to the open dumbwaiter

behind me, and don't ask where the Hanukkah _____ I just
TYPE OF FOOD

handed you came from. It's what the Howdee Doodats call "magic."

And when it comes to magic, I'm the most _____ act in town!
ADJECTIVE

I'll never forget the time I baked myself into a/an _____ of
NOUN

bread, and I'm sure neither will the American heroes I _____
VERB (PAST TENSE)

with sandwiches. I was on the cover of *Poof* _____ times,
NUMBER

and the _____ Alliance celebrated my work at the Magic
OCCUPATION

_____. I even created the video series *Use Your* _____,
NOUN NOUN

which was _____ canceled after three seasons. But possibly
ADVERB

my most _____ illusion was for my popular act, "I'm Here,
ADJECTIVE

I'm _____, And Now I'm Over Here," when I fooled the
ADJECTIVE

world into thinking I was a gay _____. Meanwhile, I
NOUN

was having a/an _____ affair with Sally _____-well *and*
ADJECTIVE VERB

my brother's widow. Don't ask me how I did it—a true magician never

reveals his _____.
PLURAL NOUN

Adult
MAD LIBS®

A POSTCARD FROM MRS. FEATHERBOTTOM

The world's greatest _family_ game

MAD LIBS® is fun to play with friends, but you can also play it by yourself! To begin with, DO NOT look at the story on the page below. Fill in the blanks on this page with the words called for. Then, using the words you have selected, fill in the blank spaces in the story. Now you've created your own hilarious MAD LIBS® game!

ADJECTIVE _____

NOUN _____

ADJECTIVE _____

NOUN _____

PART OF THE BODY _____

ADJECTIVE _____

PLURAL NOUN _____

NOUN _____

VERB ENDING IN "ING" _____

PLURAL NOUN _____

ADJECTIVE _____

VERB ENDING IN "S" _____

COLOR _____

ADJECTIVE _____

SILLY WORD _____

COLOR _____

NOUN _____

Cheerio, dearest Roger Moores, and salutations from _____
ADJECTIVE

California! It's me, your dearest _____, Felitia Featherbottom!
NOUN

Life in the Colonies is _____. Did you know Americans
ADJECTIVE

drive on the right side of the _____? And guess what they call
NOUN

a banger in the _____? A "sausage"! Mercy me! I work for
PART OF THE BODY

the most _____ family, and I feel my _____ are being
ADJECTIVE _PLURAL NOUN_

put to good use. Lady Lindsay is a real task-_____, and
NOUN

keeps me quite busy. From sunup to sundown, I am _____
VERB ENDING IN "ING"

her delicates, sweeping the _____, and caring for her
PLURAL NOUN

_____ daughter, Maeby. I've no clue where the father
ADJECTIVE

is . . . but I am sure wherever she is, she _____ them very
VERB ENDING IN "S"

much. Though my work has been rewarding, I so miss our beloved

_____-stool! But whenever I get a wee bit _____, I'll hum
COLOR _ADJECTIVE_

a little tune—hum-dee-doo-dee-_____-doo—and think of you.
SILLY WORD

If that shan't work, I shall drive to the _____-fang in Wee
COLOR

Britain, where the soup of the day is always _____.
NOUN

Yours, Felitia Featherbottom